Short Journey Upriver
Toward Ōishida

DATE DUE

D0555335

BOOKS BY ROO BORSON

Landfall 1977

In the Smoky Light of the Fields 1980

Rain 1980

A Sad Device 1981

The Whole Night, Coming Home 1984

The Transparence of November/Snow (with Kim Maltman) 1985

Intent, or the Weight of the World 1989

Night Walk: Selected Poems 1994

Water Memory 1996

*Introduction to the Introduction
to Wang Wei* (with Pain Not Bread) 2000

Short Journey Upriver Toward Ōishida 2004

Short Journey Upriver
Toward Ōishida

ROO BORSON

M&S

LIBRARY AND ARCHIVES CANADA CATALOGUING IN PUBLICATION

Borson, Roo, 1952-
Short journey upriver toward Ōishida / Roo Borson.

Poems.
ISBN 0-7710-1591-7

I. Title.

PS8553.O736S46 2004   C811'.54   C2003-906715-7

We acknowledge the financial support of the Government of Canada through the Book Publishing Industry Development Program and that of the Government of Ontario through the Ontario Media Development Corporation's Ontario Book Initiative. We further acknowledge the support of the Canada Council for the Arts and the Ontario Arts Council for our publishing program.

Typeset in Aldus by M&S, Toronto
Printed and bound in Canada

This book is printed on acid-free paper that is 100% recycled, ancient-forest friendly (100% post-consumer recycled).

McClelland & Stewart Ltd.
The Canadian Publishers
481 University Avenue
Toronto, Ontario
M5G 2E9
www.mcclelland.com

2 3 4 5   08 07 06 05 04

CONTENTS

SUMMER GRASS

Summer Grass

The willows are thinking again about thickness,
slowness, lizard skin on hot rock,
and day by day this imaging transforms them
into what we see: dragons in leaf, draped scales
alongside the river of harried, spring-stirred silt.
The magpie recites Scriabin in early morning as a mating song,
and home is just a place you started out,
the only place you still know how to think from,
so that that place is mated to this
by necessity as well as choice,
though now you have to start again from here,
and it isn't home. Venus rising in the early evening
beside the Travelodge, as wayward and causal as
will, or beauty, or as once we willed beauty to be –
though this was in retrospect, and only practice
for some other life. Do you still love poetry?
Below the willows, in the dry winter reeds,
banjo frogs begin a disconcerting raga,
one note each, the rustling blades grow green –
and it tires, the lichen-spotted tin canteen
suspended in the river weeds like a turtle
up for air: such a curious tiredness deflected there.
And what would you give up,
what would you give up, in the beautiful
false logic of math, or Greek? In the sum
of the possible, long ago in the summer grass . . .
Here beside the river I close my eyes: there
the little girls lean continuously across a rusted

sign that says Don't Feed The Swans
and feed the swans. The swans are reasoning beings;
the young cygnets, hatched from pins
and old mattress stuffing, bright-eyed, learning
what has bread, and what doesn't. What doesn't
have to do with this is all the rest:
one more chance to blow out the candles and wish
for things we wished for
that wouldn't happen unless we closed our eyes.
Not the gingko or the level gaze, or the speaking voice
beneath the pillow, or the waking in the morning
with a name. But cloud – or grief, when grief
is loneliness and you close your eyes. Speech,
when speech is loneliness, and you close your eyes.

After sickness,
light in the leaves. Dark green
and silver. All that high
heady racing in the upper keys, relentless
practice, digging down, down, Chopin, Satie –
today, in a squall, the first leaves fell.
Smell of cookies cooling on the plate;
the blue plate; some yellowing elms. And the sweet
illiterate who keeps near you as you sleep, read,
stand in line for groceries amid the bright insignia,
just to be near you, is with you now. Folly
not to actually have known them, the boy who followed
you home from school, the people dropping off
in the newspapers every day, though who
could remember the goodbyes in the exigencies
of the next life, or the glimmering half-life
of a functional lung bequeathed to a stranger? Merely to lie
tender as the rain, and the crickets
ringing beneath the eaves – *good house, good house*
they seem to say, and set to shimmering
in their patch beside the garden hose. The lone traffic
sinking, with lots of pedal, into the near distance,
a magpie maneuvering through another topologically impossible
fragment (music) – and I was wakeful,
not only with the prescience of an astute pet that knows
where home is and that we're leaving,
but something more, or it felt like more,
tinkering with faint probabilities: the sudden urge
to take up mathematics for a second time,
the premise that one might as well
get up. The residential sections were twinkling,

wobbling in the earthly atmosphere, Venus appeared
at the east window – and when dawn
sheered over the hills I could say all hesitance
had left me, for the umpteenth time had left me. Then –
facades of tinted cloud, day,
once more the long haul of outbound traffic . . .
A light rain is falling
on my way to the east. The long rain is falling,
but my heart is in the west.

If each breath is drawn from the subjunctive
now we've angled away from the sun, those Sunday morning
cartoon figures skidding on their heels toward the sudden dark
of eight p.m., so all roads lead to autumn. Wending
through a car-filled lot or the faint
verticals of a suburban wood, long declensions
of the day's events, barn owl, wisdom, vigilance,
the fibrillations – be calm, heart, hear me out.
Get the key into the ignition, gun it, and go.
Gloom is not the word, though Lutheran
sanctity would be the mood and Beethoven the season,
heading home to make dinner and a wish list
for those who'll come after: an order of things
in which to read is already to read our own minds
with better grammar. Indeed, among the clammy
clay-coated pages where you found it, among the classrooms
of dread, might still lie a secret: that you are actually,
culpably stupid, in a clinical sense. Didn't someone tell you
you have to give a little pleasure in this life
or someone might die disappointed not in you
but in themselves? The report cards with comments
are burnt in the offering, though it's hard to keep them lit:
lurid figments of a primitive time safety-sealed and mythic
as the first episodes of *Star Trek*
– or was it blood? oozing ceremoniously from some wound
until someone older noticed and thought to gasp.
Like little Genie, then, whom everybody loved
(and always so much pity), tied
to a potty chair for thirteen years (though not
her mother's pity) – led away one day,
away from that darkened room and out at last,

the next time someone hit her she lived on just the same,
though she barely spoke again. Tree rings,
parish records of the wine harvest, surviving etchings
from the Middle Ages all concur. But there's no amnesty
for ignorance or shame. Days spent standing
sentinel at the kitchen counter while the music comes in
clear and undecoded; an idea that here,
now, is a place without accolades . . .
Pedalling through the weekends' dwindling glowering rays
among motherwort and thyme, the congruences hold long enough,
a tonsure sprouts from the weeping fig in the oddness
of it, a ceaselessly climaxing unease
of salience lost along the way, cries of the honeyeater
departing the espaliered pear – you're old enough
to take solace here. As morning is
to summer, summer
to Shakespeare. And though this failure to
communicate is only partial,
and though it can't be for Genie that I write,
there is the thought of her.

Dialects of wind, water,
caesuras in the grass. Rose, meadow rue, blood-on-the-thorn
– whose tapestries delight but do not love us –
why be born? A drained windswept pool
by Eliot or Rimbaud, the plug pulled
still beside it, ludicrous and small, the tall pocked statues . . .
Elisions of winter rain, a narrow bed, a thin grey blanket –
in this, surely, must lie the contemplative life. What light
deflects through the panes at five p.m. is caramelized, like sugar –
or the snow, which would be Bach's. Voices in the blizzard:
no, no ode clothes us, but helmets and breastplates, this
or that denomination's habit of stiffened leather – milkweed,
we slip to our knees in meadows of gaunt chocolate-coloured pods,
a face appears inside the iron mask . . . What must have been
accompanies us always –

Crisp as the russet skirting of a certain dress
or the shrill algal bloom of spring nights, it was the rule:
first each boy had to help a girl into her coat
then everyone could flee into the evenings, as unalike
as those far future moments when no one could know
where we are. With the first milky creeping light and damp
peeled smell, clap of pruning shears, innumerable
Titans began to stir beneath the soil and grind their jaws.
Everything is manufactured by Mattel. If there were a hell
it would be spring, the tortures of the chrysalis,
the single suppurating hairs . . .
but it is impermissible to be excused. So I took my book
and went to lie down by an autumn stream (the leaves
that floated there were autumn's), along the way
one deciduous sunlit space which always spoke aloud –
and tried to learn how not to learn. Another set of lies,
that is. It's not the body's fault, which after all
is faithful, and loves you in its way,
but what the group mysteriously views
as its elders, viewing you as surely
you were never meant to be: intimate, pending,
to be gloated over in that terrifying
circular omniscience. Waltz. Foxtrot. The mood and rules
of the Dart Tinkham Dancing Class. From there
to summer, how far –
vistas of beach, an underwire bra and standing
around the embers under stars, stories later in the tent
that depend on voice alone, and a taste for fear –
from here, how far?

Eyes like suns on the western water, suns like eyes
or the educated song of the magpie –
If reason is a sixth sense,
does it, like the others, lie? Meeting up
by chance with the cat next door, the neighbour calling
"Gin–ger –!" the sound wafting out
on the evening air – Ginger, of course, doesn't stir.
Instead we gaze at one another unperturbed,
our cat-smiles on: once, we caught a bug together,
long ago in the summer grass. You weren't there of course,
or weren't born, though now you can come out,
come out, whoever is listening, now
that you're really you, now that you can't be anyone else.
Isn't this what we wanted after all, all those hours
with the dust motes twinkling down and the future
just detectable in the warm rays? Heavy tears are in this,
not buried deeply, but just below the sand, where fish live
with lowered heartbeats until the rains come. Heavy tears,
or shame, those same little squares that cover
the chair arms, beneath the plastic. The reasons
are inexhaustible, and thinking all the time,
like a little piece of lodestone, or the wind, which remembers
when it's in the right direction to remember. Meanwhile,
did the river move? did we die
or move away? *Eyes like suns on the western water,*
suns like eyes, or the educated song of the magpie –
goodbye, goodbye. That we gave it at least
the ritual burial of not being talked about, as it lay
forever beneath the sky on a public road.

A hand at the screen, or a moth
in the early morning dark. Which? Moon up,
everything speechless before rain. Make my way,
make my way toward the outhouse in the grey
unlikeliness –

And what if all this land, all our life,
everything we see,
should turn into a book, a story,
and never turn back again?

Dingo by the ash of last night's fire.
Two slices of white bread getting soaked.
Barramundi on the gorge wall,
waiting for rising water –

As if this
were a truer form of rapture.
And then the solstice.

River

I'm never, now, not walking by that river,
dragonflies dipped in evening sun,
coots, and the wicked swans, honking and scooting,
in the haze of after-work traffic
the whole city, it seems, setting sail for home –
home, finally, a place where we are temporarily
responsible for something: lights, water,
the neighbours' peaceful sleep, and where
another might, and will, one day, fulfill
some other function with even less ado. The planets rise
and set with all the limpid consternation the foreheads
of philosophers must feel, glowering their way
through problems they've posed themselves. Old light,
old when it reaches us. Lion-sounds from the zoo as
dusk comes on, smelling the river, no doubt –
a lament. All night the miseries of others
gnawing at our bones. But dreams
are only dreams, unless they're the dead:
elaborate in autumn's gold frame, or those resonant
kitchen sounds that let us know we're loved. Tea,
wheat, sand, water, paper, gold – a life in which,
if you pause, you can hear the dust settling,
in which summer nears winter and disappears,
each seems the only condition possible,
candid while it lasts. Bashō,
surely this is your doing.

I've been in touch with the gods,
and equally well I know
such gods do not exist. Graffiti under the bridge,
hyacinths and goslings . . . It may be
one of these so-called gods turns over in its sleep,
and so spring comes. The moral order of minerals,
the code of the samurai in stone. For ague:
read the old books in which ague is still argued.
For sun, for rain: a pink umbrella. But in the cool
of the rain you'll be on your own, though the evening
is upright and sharp and the petals scatter,
don't imagine I'll come after you, for I'll be gone –
lingering among the heliotrope,
or stuck to the sole of your shoe,
where again you won't know me. And when the pages,
cool and soft, intend a melody, remember
you weren't here before and you won't be again,
when you go the whole world goes with you,
trace of an afterimage in the infrared
measured by some lonely instrument in Baja.
As I write this, clouds are being born,
they blow across the sky at dawn.
Infinite patience, infinite
disinclination to understand. Just so,
it will be early again, in the faint blue realms.

Greetings of strangers in the morning
and again at evening, people out walking,
or else walking their dogs, a formal brevity
in such mere pleasures. Though when the wind
blows in from the hot dusty centre and a harsh
arguing ascends, the petty dicta can be seen
standing whole, for a moment, in the sky above the trailer park,
the illumined ends of our need for reason
falling to the river, glittering ash. No, pure heart,
you're not the only poetry, though you may be the best,
at least against the summer's heat. Here
at the bottom of the world the whorls
of weather are as big as a continent,
July is in January, so January is in July,
and the cool change comes, when it comes,
from the coast. *In the sum*
of the beautiful I closed my eyes and lay down,
the god of spring at my cheek,
and the summer gods,
and the four hundred gods of the summer night skyline.
All six thousand miles of me I laid down,
nerves and blood and faeces –
lay down, eyes closed,
where the god of poetry is poetry.

        Long river,
I do still long for you. To make
these drifting things,
of cast-offs
dribbled down the banks in fealty to something
not well understood, like deities perhaps,
a twisted shirt,
a bottle a house in turn atop the reeds,
things for coots and insects to use, if they choose to.

        So much
        for logic.

Spring, I'll say, *coming all this way*
just to see me again, here or on the road –
but in the mornings when you've gone off to work
a loneliness moves into the litter on the hillside
as if it could replace you. Hardly anyone knows this.
No arguments, no dicta, but the little yard intact.

        And the life beneath this life?

Rivers to the Sea

From rain to underground springs, from springs
to fountains, freshets, and rivers,
from rivers to the sea, or the winter snow.
But the wind, *the wind bloweth where it listeth,*
like those disjunct souls drifting and alighting,
always distant – spaceships, or glowing teacups,
most often seen at dusk, on the long straight stretches.
What message? Just that no one any longer
means to do you any harm, or good,
though the dog and then the cat come in,
each able to grant a single wish in exchange for which
each would be the star of the household.
Now the seasons are merely vestigial,
though what shrivels the leaves still fattens the eels,
autumn too – cluttering the playground with extra fins and tails
after everyone's gone home to tomato soup and toast.
Lost in the wood like Hindemith. Whosoever's children
are not practising now will never learn their instruments –

But gentle as the Thursday rain
or the winged sound of traffic as the bakeries are closing
toward four p.m. and there never was, nor can be,
any other form of waking life: now,
goes the ancient advice, is the time for practising
the character for courage. But what if the strokes
are hesitantly drawn, a lost direction,
yellow bedstraw or cloth of gold,
in the nether months, in the nether weeks of the year?
What then are the obligations? Torrens, Patawalonga,
Onkaparinga. Little Para, Torrens. Early or late
along the river road. The leaves are streaked with brilliantine,
the pelicans to their estuaries, the coots to their
twigs and bottle. What are the obligations?
From springs to fountains, fountains to rivers, rivers to the sea.
Button grass or couch grass in the fallen yellow light.
Black silk pool, mirror of no thoughts –
black silk mirror, river of no thoughts.

    To set off, instead, on a May morning,
as convention dictates, whether south or north,
autumn or spring, the commentaries decline to tell us.
But the line bends as the river bends, the cherries of that
other time are pink and dark and sweet, an allegorical painting
standing in for the world in the level light of dawn,
morning along the river, growing warm. Who lives here?
Herons standing sentry, bees in the bee tree at noon.
To live to tell old news, without the disgust the dead must feel
toward portraiture, or music – harmonics that depend,
as always, on previous conditions. Anyway,
to change pitch continuously
might be one aim.

Solstice

As for you, world –
you'll have become small, and round, and lavender-coloured: ode
to the ewer, the comb, the water cooler.
And you? You lived in a place which was once a town,
you've seen it on maps before, others loaded ships
as in a dream: mood, appetite, memory, learning –
the demands seemed endless, all marsh-lights and loveliness,
the final estimates for the real world
or these propositions, for instance, which are sometimes true.
Indeed such unconscious concentration is possible,
in the neon light of early spring
and later, those evenings no longer fully spring
yet not quite summer either,
when the scent pulls back into the flower
and blackbirds bathe among violets,
half aspect, half unreal, in the slow rain of leaves.
Day after day, some days not returning,
and the boughs painted with light green lichen,
the detailed pink of the flowering apricot –
don't go there unless to banish yourself,
because you *are* banished, beech,
oak, birch, and yew, among the hazel woods
of the elder world, where feathers flash
among the branches and hide in the darkening varnish
and history becomes the history of bad ideas,
a gloom of rotten nuts and nut-skins,
bitter paper. And tonight
the half-light in which paper glows –

walls, porticos, arches, palaces (who lived there?),
the print invisible, and the ocean sounding
all night long, clavicle to *vena cava*,
clavicle to *vena cava*,
it's not a description.

Then the dye runs,
and it's summer. Sky blue to blue,
and the flowers come out in kind –
there was so much time back then, spare time,
that even now is never wholly gone.
A trip upriver to inspect the river gods:
sunlight, nightfall, the grasses tall beside the water,
at dusk the buildings lit up with names. A book, a tune –
there isn't even a word for it in English,
but a day in the summer house, someone dressing up
in the spirit of wisteria. Do you hear it? Footfalls
in the garden, or no it's the rain
eking out the hours til dawn,
the moth in the midnight toilet, afloat in death
when all are sleeping –
and then once more the sleepers
lie scattered in sleep,
butterflies tumbling down a stone road,
lovers holding up their hair –
Sentient and insensate gods, genus of surfaces,
are you sleeping?

    But summer is gone now,
and would not know you. Lost? Follow a river.
Heron, night heron. To see by seeing,
or else to see the things that music says, and means,
and cannot mean, in the reddish evening light,
somewhere in the world where what you love
is also loved. Saint-Saëns. The days are gone
in sleep and daydream, first the black notes,
then the white, the notes both sung and heard
– not really there. And what would you give up?
Ink, snow, sweat, spring –
how kind you all are to come see me again –
disordered gentleness, winter,
you blue girl . . .
all the ordered waters of the world
spontaneous and permanent –
or just the lazy snow.
And so to have to choose.
Soon, soon, like those fisher birds
that live along the riverland, bees in the bee tree –

    Bashō, is that you again?
    Voice of rain
    on the banana leaves –

The beautiful false premise. The night, the daylight.

AUTUMN RECORD

Yoshino
cherries:
autumn
in the underworld.

It was March, the beginning of autumn in the southern hemi-sphere, and we had just seen Yoshino cherries – the famous trees, that is – for the first time. Except this wasn't Yoshino, and they weren't blossoming. Instead the leaves were a dry late-summer green, even after the drizzle that had come and gone, alternating with fog, all day. Walking high up along the path that threads one side of the ravine, black dripping foliage below, dry sky above, there was a clear sense of being in two places at once: two continents, two ideas, each a museum and a wilderness. Yoshino and Mt. Lofty. Later that night, under the reading lamp, for a moment my eyes close: light of another day, crickets singing in the long daylight grass.

Often now by the river there are fragments of dead things, some-times no more than a couple of shining fish scales, or a tail unattached to anything. This week so far I've seen a whole duck carcass that had been mauled and started to blacken, and something else: the picked-clean skeleton of a tiny nestling – though when I crouched down beside it, it seemed to be made of fish bones. My eyes, even my teeth, are not what they used to be – so whatever I say now I have to say with a lisp.

All night possums on the roof
play leaping sliding games –
and now the rain.

I try to think of what it must be like – to have a mating season,
like the brushtail possums. We're watching television with the lights out
when the thunder begins on the roof: galloping, followed by a drawn-
out rhythmic wheezing, wild and strange. Then they leap into the trees
and are gone. All day long the persistent sense of descending damp
concrete stairs; leaf tips, rooftops, can be all alight with afternoon sun,
yet we're in an underworld. Rooms at night so completely dark there is
neither right nor left, no past or future. Lifting back the curtain, there
might be a dot of light – but this too, whatever is visible, is just another
temperature of the one monotonous dimension, which is darkness.

A forensic gloom of hairs, leaves, pollen, petals, fur, burrs, seeds, segments of casuarina, the dusky red threads of the bottlebrush. Every day the carpets accumulate new decorations, beside which the shoes take on a festive air, having fetched them in. Certain plants are only now coming into flower: new candles on the sawtooth banksias, bursts of red and yellow in the eucalypts. Yesterday an elderly man on the bus had a minute green flower caught in his hair. It must have fallen from a tree as he passed under it.

To learn from an old master might be better –
but there's only the brimming grass,
the young river.

How easily last year's growth, some of it over twelve feet high,
simply slumps toward the ground and is gone. And now the new
unruly grass, a brilliant green along the banks. I found a baby bird, all
skin and skeleton, no feathers yet, gawky as a young turkey but no
more than three inches long, shivering at the edge of the path. It
couldn't walk, would tip over if it tried, its beak heavier than its legs. All
the adult birds were off on the river, paying no attention. Coots and
swans, pelicans, navy-chested swamp-hens. I scooped up the orphan
with a magazine and carried it to the zoo nearby, where a keeper was
called. Instantly she took it into her hands, crooning over it, then just as
quickly scolded me, saying I'd have to take it back to the spot where I'd
found it, that all I could do now was to leave it by the river again with
its human scent.

Saturdays are market days. Beautiful white cheeses in wheels and semicircles. Chunks of the pumpkin they call "blue" because of its softly glossy bluish skin, a complexion roughened by buff-coloured seams and patches. Garlic chives, and varieties of green and purple water-plants that take their bitterness from the mineralized water in which they anchor themselves and grow. The high roof of the block-long market building protects everything under it: sheepskins, boots, cans of coconut milk and jars of mayonnaise, breads baked in the shapes of loaves and turtles, used television sets that may or may not work when you plug them in, huge proteas, lavishly silvered with furry edging, standing in plastic buckets. Above the best of the apple stands (Fuji and still-green Golden Delicious from the cooler hills outside the city), a boobook owl has taken shelter on one of the thick crossbeams. It sleeps, eyes shut, its flat clock-face utterly calm amidst the hubbub of the market (though one imagines the quiet of nighttime when the gates will be locked, and mice dare to crisscross the expanse for bits of fallen food), the bigger vegetable stalls with their callers, each one louder and auctioning off the remainders at lower prices than the next, "Everything fifty cents but me!" and offering slices of overripe melon or bruised peach.

There are days when everything seems to be in parables. Reflections draped along the river, a young tree half in autumn, half in spring, (I don't know what kind) – pink-veined blossoms on the one side, dried burgundy leaves on the other – shaking in the wind. It seems the seasons here confuse all but the native species, this tree joining the jacarandas, which have flowered for the third time in a single year. I can find no evidence of grafting on the young trunk, no scar. The fleshy blossoms on the half-tree's naked boughs are reminiscent of spring, but only as an emblem is reminiscent, or a keepsake by which one is still implicated in the events of one's past. Certainly nothing like the rafts of cherry and plum which, filling the eyes in springtime, can temporarily blind us.

Instead a faint thrill, that old feeling of dread over the simplest things.

Finally the rain comes, strumming the roof.
Two or three letters in the letterbox.

The new calendar? Same pictures as last year.

You can always tell the first real rain of autumn. Even if it's only the first few drops, they announce themselves by resonating a little more hollowly, and that much more resolutely, demonstrating that summer has indeed been broken and will not be returning. As the dark falls earlier and earlier, whatever had been shrugged off among the summer drinks and gaiety as if it were some ghost of private idealism, not only outmoded but useless, comes back now with renewed longing. Home, security, permanence. A society structured on kindness. Friendship undisfigured by envy.

Eighth anniversary of my mother's death.
I warm myself
in her red mittens.

Today I waited out a rainstorm under an umbrella at an outdoor café. The place was deserted except for several crows – fanning and folding their wings, and in that way too staying dry in the rain.

Lately I've come across a curious sort of litter, scattered widely and evenly beneath a certain stand of pines. Not just needles, though there are dry needles underneath, but bits and pieces of shredded cone. And now I see that overhead, cockatoos, each balancing on one foot among the boughs, grasping a chewed-off cone in the other, are eating ripe pine seeds, shredding the tough cones with their tough-as-nails bills, and in the process littering the path below. Farther along a car has been pushed halfway into the river. It must have taken at least two people to accomplish this: the reeds all around it are flattened. A policeman and police dog emerge from the riverbank where they've been searching, and head off into the flowering wasteground along the old rail line, bottles and cans aglint beneath the net of purple morning glories.

Policeman and police dog, on duty:
neither returns my smile.

Once, early in the morning, I happened upon a few drops of still-wet blood. This was on the university grounds, and I could see a broken ground-floor window in a nearby building. I followed the trail, the drops getting smaller and farther apart as I went, all the way to the State Library, where they simply stopped. Things like this happen in broad daylight, when help is nowhere near. Another time, not far from here, I came upon someone crouched in the shadows beneath the overpass. He stood up with his pants down, not even bothering to wipe himself, and looked straight into my face.

Going through clothes that haven't been touched
since the final weeks of early spring –

I find wads of tissue,
tickets to performances I'd forgotten we attended.

Rain, then a dust storm (those of us unlucky enough to be waiting for the bus shield our eyes by leaning into the back of the person ahead of us in line) – followed by innumerable minute white flies which must have hatched all at once or else been carried by the wind in the wake of the cyclone which, the late-afternoon news tells us, has destroyed two towns in the far northwest. They settle in the backyard pomegranate tree, and rise and shift and settle again as the gusts wane. The cats, usually so disdainful of surprises, explore with barely trembling steps their changed circumstances.

The leaves of the ornamental plums and apricots, the plane trees, the various deciduous imports and fruit trees, are finally down. The city looks newly swept. No one about (it's Sunday), but an empty phonebox outside the Mobil station keeps ringing and ringing.

Today I enter a room in which the people I've known who are dead now are lined up as figurines on a mantelpiece facing the wall, no more than a foot high, made of some hard substance, wood or pottery, each with an arm bent upward at the elbow, fingers raised in some symbolic configuration, whose meaning, it is clear, is inaccessible to me.

On waking, though, what seems most strange is that there was no fire in the hearth.

I had never expected poetry to provide for anything beyond itself, but now I feel unhappy with poetry – or with myself – for not exceeding those expectations. The feeling is the feeling of reaching the end of Montale's poems to his dead wife just as it's becoming too dark to read, the lights coming on in the city below just as the stars too are coming out, as you wait for someone you love and depend on to be finished with some chore and come back with the car. The grasses are tasselled with seed, the crickets beginning, in stops and starts, suggestive trills. All of this happens in memory of course, recalled under the lamp's warmth as you lie in bed with your eyes closed, too tired to read. Later they'll sound more insistent: exploratory, expository, epistolary, before becoming exhausted.

"After prose has said all it can, or at least all that it is decent for it to attempt, poems rise to have their say." (Earl Miner, translator and commentator.) The Japanese, still writing in classical Chinese while adapting literature to their own purposes, were the first to compose poetic diaries. But there's only so much that even poetry can attempt. As the weeks go on, the crickets begin singing in the daytime too, as though wearying, or muddled, looking straight into daytime's true face as though it were darkness.

And where, in all of this, is autumn?

"Does it reside in the ink? But the ink is used up." (Chu Lu, painter.)

"All dark lines, and subordinate subjects of regret." (From another dream.)

The poems rise up (now, as then), but the feeling isn't in poetry.

> When no one is present,
> but it appears that someone is present,
> autumn is here.

PERSIMMONS

We had been driving in the hills in a borrowed car for the day when the road took a steep downhill curve, and we entered into a small vale. Houses stood here and there closed in by trees, many of which were fruit trees and had kept their leaves longer than any I'd noticed in the hills that day or in the city. Neither the wind nor the strong autumn light seemed able to penetrate this place, though it had rained: there were bright damp yellows and a few flaps of red against the black trunks. It couldn't have taken more than a few seconds to round the last narrow curve up and out, yet what flashed past at that moment is still with me. It was a house, nothing more – with a persimmon tree in front of it.

The tree was huge, and entirely bare of leaves, but there were still a hundred or so fruits hung like glowing lanterns from the slender boughs. Behind it stood the house, of two or three storeys, a discoloured white stucco with lead-light windows which would have looked out onto the tree and the road. The tree had been regularly pruned and the small bulb garden recently attended to, yet the house gave off such a sensation of abandonment – though under what circumstances it had been abandoned, it was impossible to tell.

The gloom, the empty house, the persimmons glowing under their stretched skins though no one was there to pick them: it was an image of death for me, not of my own but of my mother's, and of the life I had lived up until her death. It brought to mind Tanizaki's story "Arrowroot," which I'd read some years earlier.

In the story, the narrator agrees to accompany a friend upriver, toward his mother's ancestral village. The friend, having been raised by relatives, had barely known his mother, and now, in journeying upriver, was trying to find out something of the truth of her circumstances. Along the way, they stop to visit the head of a poor family whose only treasures are the possibly faked antiquities which have brought a modicum of prestige to the area over the years, among them a scroll and a fox-skin drum. The drum was the more famous of the two, and for good reason: the skins originally used to cover it were said to have come from two foxes that had once been people – or so, at least, went the story as I remembered it. In the mythology of the region, the white fox Myōbu-no-shin is associated with the harvest god Inari, and can be summoned at will by those with the talent for it. Like the Lady Shizuka in the play *The Thousand Cherry Trees* – though in that case it is the presence of the drum, and his desire to be near his parents, that draws the fox Tadanobu on, and brings him into proximity with humans. In Tanizaki's story, the friend, directed finally to the family home, arrives to find a girl of maybe eighteen outside making paper. It is here that he first begins to discover some of the details he has been seeking. It seems his mother's father, in some reversal of fortune no longer recorded, was forced to sell his daughter into bondage in the pleasure quarters of Ōsaka. That same grandfather, it turns out, was said to have once "summoned foxes."

I'd been reminded once before of Tanizaki's story, shortly after my father's death. On an isolated sandspit along the far northwest coast, a red fox had trotted nonchalantly past, as if to mimic the Hiroshige print my father had hung on the wall of his consulting room. Now it was as if the story of the fox-skins, and those persimmons, had been waiting to haunt me, ever since my mother, too, had died, and the world, without my parents, had become a hollow place.

For most of my adult life, even in the midst of the busiest public market, I've had to turn away, with a ridiculous anguish, from the sight of persimmons. Two persimmon trees had grown in my mother's garden. But it was through the description of the persimmons offered by the villagers as an autumn refreshment in Tanizaki's story that I'd recognized the ones I'd eaten as a child. They too must have been of the Mino variety.

It's hardly worth describing these trees in any season other than autumn. It's against autumn's enamelled blue skies that the oval leaves begin to turn, first leathery, then increasingly brittle, as if glazed with egg-white, while beneath the polished surface a variegated gleam, almost like that of fire opals, rises. And the fruits, the dull green of young bamboo when small, grow slowly until they are of a size to sit squarely in the palm. It's at this point that they should be picked: a frosty orange colour, with the blush of powder still on them. For some reason the tree farthest from the house always set fruit earlier and bore the most. The nearer tree, presumably hampered by the extra hour of shade cast as the sun turned the corner of the house, never seemed to grow as sturdy as the other, and its fruits, too, remained small. It stood there under the gaze of the back bedroom where my mother would sometimes nap of an afternoon, overlooking the garden.

It was my job to check the picked fruits day by day, to select and serve them to family and guests in persimmon season, but it was my mother's gardener, George, who looked after picking them. George came on Wednesdays. It was my parents' day off, and though my father would always have patients to attend to in the hospital, my mother could spend all morning with her hair undone at the dining table, idling through the newspaper. Her patients were women, and apart from the occasional call to deliver a child, most surgery, as well as regular appointments, could be scheduled for other days.

Mid-morning, George would knock on the glass door of the plant room, which was adjacent to the dining room, and my mother would rise in her kimono-sleeved dressing gown to accompany him on their weekly rounds of the garden. Together they'd lean in consultation over a bonsai, or some other to-others-invisible problem, or they'd inspect the fishpond from a distance, all the while delicately colluding, sorting out priorities for the day or the season. Despite her profession, my mother was naturally so shy as to appear aloof, and to compensate spoke in loud imperious tones. Yet here she was a gentler person, more herself. Her voice was audible, if not her words – though not once was

I able to catch a hint of George's replies, which were apparently so understated that even the breeze failed to carry them for any distance. They moved as one around the garden, propelled through a world apart from us, an extra-familial world, where she relied without question on his expertise. He was originally from Japan, and perhaps found English difficult, or perhaps because they communicated only about such topics as they both had intimate knowledge of, little explanation was needed – as though a tendril of ivy were itself a sentence, or a flower a burst of sentient feeling. Neither old nor young, with his slight stoop he seemed a scrupulously modest man, noiselessly moving the wooden ladder around, weeding tirelessly, tying the spent irises into knots, or twisting persimmons from overladen branches.

I was not yet twelve when, one July, playing 'grass fairies' under the sprinklers, I slipped on the slick lawn. The wind knocked out of me, an ankle twisted awkwardly, I could neither move nor breathe. The glittering veils I'd skipped through only a moment before now passed over me mechanically. The next moment the water was shut off. George appeared, looking quickly into my pained face, though we'd never so much as exchanged a word. And then my parents were there, carrying me into the house. I spent the rest of the summer in a cast up to my knee. It was about this time that I began to feel queasy about boys, and in the autumn, too, my body began to change.

Most days, standing on the ladder, George would find only a few fruits to his liking; these he could fit into the pockets of his khakis. But as the season wore on, he'd have to descend several times to empty them onto a canvas tarp. Then he'd carry them to the plant room – really an enclosed porch glassed-in on two sides – which on a sunny day had the enervating atmosphere of a hothouse. Here my mother grew orchids and staghorn ferns and bromeliads; here too the smaller garden tools were kept, shears and trowels and diggers of various sorts, adding a metallic note to the fragrance of pebbles and peat moss. At the height of persimmon season as many as nine crates might be stacked in sets of three on the plant-room floor. But the fruits, which bruise easily, could only be accommodated in a single layer, necessitating much movement of crates as well as of individual fruits, which would ripen unpredictably, and therefore had to be examined each day.

At the early stages it is possible to gauge the ripeness of a persimmon by sight, but once the skin begins to turn translucent all finer judgment must rely on touch. I had taken it upon myself to remember who, among the members of my family, preferred them just 'gelled' – translucent but still firm and buttery – and who liked them fully ripened, with a blowsy fragrance that meant a clear orange-flecked water would seep from the fruit the instant it was touched by a knife. But that fall, sent to the plant room to select dessert for a number of guests seated at the dining table, all of whom could see me through the French doors as I crouched, one after the other slowly palpating the persimmons, I felt myself flush, and turned my back to them.

About this time too I began to go to a rarely used place to be alone. The area under the wooden staircase at the front of the house was a narrow enclosure, tall at one end, and there was a rickety door you could pull to. Hoses were stored here, and faucets could be turned on or off for watering various parts of the garden. It smelled of dirt and concrete, snails sometimes strayed in, and sunlight and shadow alternated in severe stripes cast by the slatted stairs. At a younger age I'd been afraid of this place: monstrous things lived there, fictions of the slatted light, reaching out their spindly arms as I and my playmates raced up the stairs and into the house. Now the damp half-darkness seemed a haven. I did nothing much – hugged my knees, or watched for spiders. It didn't occur to me until the moment the door swung open that this would be one of George's places too: from here he could enter the basement to get the larger shovels or the long-handled cherry-picker, and in fact it must have been from here that he'd shut off the water when I'd slipped on the lawn. We might have exchanged a nod or smile, and so with a certain awkwardness glossed over our mutual startlement, but instead, instantly and somehow admirably, without a word, he backed off and shut the door.

Not long afterwards George returned to Japan. Maybe there were ailing relatives, or an opportunity for work now that the economy had recovered somewhat after the war. It could have been sheer homesickness. In any case, it took my mother some time to reconcile herself to the loss. For a few years occasional handyman-gardeners drifted in and out, having advertised their services on telephone poles around the neighbourhood. The garden languished, as did my mother's mood and bearing, one always reflecting the other. It was only when I returned home from college for a visit that I found the garden, and my mother, restored to something like their earlier state. The new gardener was from Mexico. "Whore-Hey –" my mother would call after him, screwing her mouth into a hideous grimace in the conscientious attempt to pronounce his name – and so Jorge too, at his own insistence, became "George." Once he had been a high-school Spanish teacher; now he was a gardener, and carver. Whistling buoyantly wherever he went, he added coriander and tomatillo to beds that had once held only irises and quince.

There comes a point in the lifetime of any garden when the garden is at its peak – and this point arrived just as my mother's life was waning. Since the death of my father she had ventured outdoors less and less, finally turning away even from the windows. She died in a long purple nightgown, the purple of a clematis that had once climbed the front of the house. She died on my father's side of the bed, where she'd been sleeping since his death.

"These nights, to get to sleep, I imagine a bullet entering the back of my head," reads the start of a diary I kept at the time. The first night I spent alone in that house it was full of such abandonment it seemed no one should try to sleep there ever again. I spent the days burning stacks of old magazines in the fireplace, carting out troves of glass jars and newspapers. But the worst part was clearing out the fridge: the bits of food she was no longer there to eat. Several dozen containers of coffee-flavoured yogurt, practically the only thing she'd been able to get down for months. Two Brown 'N Serve sausages, by now covered in 'hoarfrost,' at one end of a near-empty package that had very likely been there for years. I fried them up and choked them down straight from the pan, burning my mouth. And in the months that followed what hurt most were the simple things: coming across a brand of bread she would have liked, or an imported fruit she'd never be able to taste.

After she was cremated we held a simple ceremony in the garden, planting her ashes with my father's beneath the redwood trees. A week or so afterwards a hand-carved cross appeared there, and we knew who had made it. I wished the original George too could have stood with us once more, in the garden he helped create. The first person to disappear from one's life, having been there from at least as far back as memory is able to reach, always occupies a special place, just as a first lover does. The disappearance remains eerie, a foretaste, inexplicable. Still, in hindsight, George's disappearance is not nearly so eerie as the fact that he had once been there: that a grown man, and one with such skills as he had, would be forced by circumstance to leave behind everything he had known – land, language, family – and to replace all of it, even his name, merely to work in my mother's garden. For "George" was of course no more his name than it was Jorge's. Once the property had been sold and my brothers had divided up the ashes and buried them elsewhere, the cross remained.

And then, years on, we came across the house in the little glade, with its tree full of ripe persimmons, and its echoes. "After three days one eats again; after three months one washes again; after a year one wears raw silk again under the garment of mourning." So Confucius is said to have said. It's only now, another two years after passing through that dark persimmon glade, that I can look on persimmons – ridiculous as it sounds – with equanimity. It seems a shame that such fruit, of which there was once such an abundance, and for free, is now to be bought only at great cost, and that the fruits are not only expensive but inferior, picked too soon, scarred by shipping. I would like to go back and look at the house in the little glade, but it isn't mine, and people may be living in it after all. Neither have I gone back to my ancestral home in all these years: though I've lost all rights to that place, I would rather not have to see others living there. I suppose it would have been no different had I ventured upriver with Tanizaki in autumn. Fox-skin drums, persimmons. Either would have been shown up for what it was: overvalued, esteemed only by villagers who have no other object of their pride, and by the odd traveller or two, seeking refreshment, who discover, not entirely by accident, some deep familial connection to the place.

WATER COLOUR

. . . after that I decided I could go back to school on the island, i.e. study colour much more carefully, see if I could become more subtle with it. So each day when I go over on the ferry I watch the colours of the water, the sky, the islands, the trees, the brush, the grasses, and try to print my brain with what colours were salient that morning . . .

GARDEN

A bridge, a stream, someone's careless foot,
and all the slender mushrooms
at the edge of the path are toppled.

    This upside-down yellow leaf
    sails the moss,
    stem lifted.
    Stern too.

Say goodbye to bye to bye to – what?
Birds in the cedar,
which I've never seen.

    Zigzag bridge,
    arrowroot thriving where irises once grew –
    or did they?

Eye of the lake
half-closed with ice.
Ducks at the one end, sleeping.

    Autumn passes by, still speaking
    with an older accent,
    like my teacher's –

Star moss, holding aloft . . . what?
'Star,' 'roots,' 'tar,' and 'moss' –
my head is spinning!

Seen here,
this person in tennis shoes, head bent,
studying some pages.
Monk's robes in a world
where there are no monks anymore.

Teahouse with no tea.
Alcove whose waiting bench is waiting –
only no one comes.
Floor swept. Not one stray leaf.
Not even me.

Small moth
from the maple woods
outside the garden:
you turn out to be
a seed.

Waterfall
in
autumn.
Twig broom
leaned against the teahouse wall.

Going the
'wrong way'
round the garden –
how wild it seems –

SPRING CHERRIES

All night, bending
over my back fence: spring.
My neighbour's cherry tree.

    No need to go far today.
    Just these dandelions
    staring down the sky.

Like Saigyō then.
Wandering cold among the blossoms
after night falls –

    The blossoming cherry
    so alight outside my window
    I can read his poems by it.

A poem about a robin – yes,
but that was long ago,
and I was young and foolish. Saigyō,

    now I blush, and so become the colour of that robin,
    to have been so
    "insufficiently impressed."

Suddenly the depths: the morning fresh,
but overcast. Wild honeysuckle,
colours of dawn, all day.

Easy to forget
how sick I used to feel
each spring –

This morning, wanting to shut myself away
even from blossoms – my father's child, as they used to say.
And then those blossoms (knock at the door)
splashed against my neighbour's fence –

A package. First me, then the delivery man –
spring light
looking out
from our faces.

The man around the corner
who used to come out to bother me
must be ill now. As I pass, he calls out weakly
Hey girl –

Soon I'll be fifty.
Around the block, another cherry tree.
Another's cherry tree. Like it I want to begin
blossoming first from the very tips.

I think of them again:
all those years tramping the sidewalks –
tramping the sidewalks, sometimes finding just the right present!

Wanting to shut myself away even from blossoms,
this year
the date of my father's birthday came round again.

First, snow
milling about the house,
then petals –
inside: this great dumb winter fly.

Saigyō, is that you?
In the early-morning dark,
lilac breeze through the window,
summer storm behind that –

SUMMER RIVER

All along the summer river,
this confused heart –
wild anise and pine.
It's not a place for rest,
and not for meditation –
It's a place of endless daydreams,
something flowing underneath reflections on the water.

If you come down to the summer river,
what is it you'll eat? Clouds, ducks –
reflections of ducks, wild anise and pine.
The river will eat you or spit you out.
Now: not looking at the river, what are you?

Whatever people say I can't remember.
Trying to get it right I stumble on.
"O cadets of river-shadow –"
and the words arrive.
All night the words arrive like horses, horses
that are gone, and then it's morning.

Only weeks ago, two of them.
Two stilt-birds, each standing on one leg side by side.
Now, day after day, just one of them comes to stand by the river
and at night returns to the nearby sports-field
to stand alone until dawn.
Is it his loneliness
I feel, or my own?

Now if I come close,
he hobbles away.
Trying to keep him company,
I force him from the shade.
Grown boys tussle, toss balls around,
they're in college.
He stands at the edge of the world
and waits – or not – for his "friend" to return.

In the morning I wake and find that pity in myself again,
every day dream of this or that.
That's what the river's good for:
flowing, taking away.

The miner birds get to harry the magpies.
The magpies close in around the rattletrap doves.
The rattletrap doves run away from footsteps.
The footsteps come to the ginger flowers and stop,
but the ginger flowers don't notice.

So here they are,
in the joints of bamboo:
the poems I meant to write.

– A type of banana tree
that shares Bashō's name:
its trunk a dull bronze mirror
filled with water long ago.

It's not a place of daydream,
and not for meditation.
For the crane and the cormorant
it's a place to catch fish.
Try to meditate here
and you'll soon be carried off.
The river has no breath in it but it ripples.

Almost afternoon,
and the ducks still sleeping.
Late in the summer
the river closes over.
Dragonflies, leaves
drift all one way –
all leaves, no reflections.

Friends talk about "empathy,"
and I talk back.
We keep drinking, the conversation veers off.
Awake, alone, I lie awake.
All night the argument continues.

The bay tree smells of my old home,
or is it just a past that's truly past?
The moon is a rock that doesn't move.
The egret, only whiteness
rippling on the water.
Give me another world –
one made of grass,
cicadas,
the crying in the grass.

A bug flies past. Flies past,
and I understand
what it is to be born.
Next life, I'll love you again –

The daydream river,
smell of sunwarmed pine.
Talking to myself again –
why wouldn't I tell the truth?
What I dreamed of
a moment ago.
For a moment,
when I thought I had no other life.

GREEN WORLD

Today I killed the spider
that had been resting on the lampshade
while I read –

Midday heat,
the cool look
a scrap of paper gives.

Blinds drawn,
the house a lantern
unlit from within.

Summer after summer,
the hills covered with golden straw,
the same buzz-saw came back to life.

I'm like a toy that lies all day,
bad-tempered in the grass, and then the next morning
is found there, unrepentant, covered in dew.

Down in the cool basement, in the old trunk,
after all these years, I came across my old doll.
She lay there looking up at me, as if still covered in dew, forlorn.

My thoughts now
are for the small cat
that died in the night.

My neighbour found it lying in the grass:
"One of the wild kittens –"
dead.

I heard something cry out in the night
and woke with a start. Room
like a black-and-white photo,

    my companion still asleep beside me,
    streetlight through the open window
    casting his shadow on the bed.

My neighbour
set the remains of breakfast outside
in a skillet in the grass this morning.

    Crying, she said "The little cats . . ."
    And I remembered how she was before – that other time,
    after her mother died. Mine too.

Now I can hear her
in the backyard,
shaking out the printed sheets again.

    What is rain if it isn't rain?
    Or autumn, autumn. Spring, spring.
    The summer rain.

Today I killed the spider
that had been resting on the lampshade while I read,
morning glories appeared at our common fence,

flowers so profuse I couldn't rest,
mind racing –
what is it for?

At the first sign of overcast,
an insect, wings black as oil,
hovers at my window.

First water, then a willow, rippling. Open book.
House like a bellows.
Someone knocking at my front door.

SEVEN VARIATIONS ON THE WORD SILK

In the middle of my life,
I've made new friends, and come at last to think kindly of the Dao.
The city I used to know is still there,
but the person I was is not.

I'd forgotten what it's like – this kind of autumn –
big melon-coloured leaves everywhere,
the last of the blackberries, "Eat some for me" –
bicyclist riding past.

The mind is a horse I want to learn to ride again,
but this time, properly –
the landscape suddenly unfurling,
like a painted scroll on raw silk.

My days are simple now:
open my purse for pen and paper,
put them away. Open it up,
put them away again.

Every year the cool heart of early autumn comes.
I'm like a bird that should have long since headed south –
fall asleep in the afternoon,
forget to write poetry.

Clean the house,
let the dust gather.
Smile at people out walking.
Someone's dog smiles back.

My love is away
and a long-legged spider
shares the shower. Old books,
old grocery lists still holding my place.

> Leaf after leaf
> unfolding in my teacup –
> as if I might still find spring there.

These days are days like any other,
a spider's thread caught in sunlight,
boredom tangled in the spindles
of the afternoon.

> Yellow leaves, some clinging,
> some fallen.
> Standing on the path,
> lost as usual –

dog sniffing my shoes.
Steps aside,
sneezes.
Then a light rain.

> Under the pink umbrella, waiting,
> the world brightens, then floats.
> *First Fuji, then toward Ueno –*
> What am I thinking of?
> A bridge, or station?
> Somewhere in Japan.

In the wind that arrives before nightfall,
the leaves sunlit for an afternoon, I wonder sometimes
what to do with them?
The taste of pears, the smell of ivy.

Red-maple keys hanging on,
and a spare key to my apartment, freshly cut.

Someone's penny, lost on the subway floor,
the autumn bark of the once-flowering cherry.

Clouds tearing past over the city,
new friends (as I've said)
with a taste for congee and sea bass.

I chose writing
because it is secret. Now – more dogs,
one of them (how polite)
lowering his eyes as I pass.

Night getting cold, no frost.
Geese swinging north
on their way to the south.

Feathered seeds everywhere
issuing from some nameless plant.

Small birds (winter wrens?)
quick in the blackberry thatch.

Black page, lit, where
sunlight gets in around the edges.

A golden caterpillar!
Now the whole world.

A BIT OF HISTORY

"Dreams are the great literature of nighttime." This fragment of what seemed to be a poem, or epigraph, or possibly an admonition, came back to me suddenly as if from the dream I'd been having – though it could also have come from the story I'd finished reading before falling asleep, a translation of "Ashizuri Point" by Tamiya Torahiko, a writer I'd never heard of before. The story had been written in the 1930s about a place in Japan where it was so common to commit suicide that the town set aside a yearly sum for recovering the bodies of those who had jumped from the cliffs into the sea. This despite the legend, circulated among would-be suicides, that the bodies of those who leap from the cliffs at Ashizuri Point sink like stones and are never recovered. The contradictory information presented two pictures, one fanciful, one factual; one romantic, one practical – though it's not necessarily easy to decide which adjective should be applied to which picture. Looking back through the story, I could find no remnant of the phrase, which isn't to say it isn't there, only that when I looked I couldn't find it.

I'd just come back from a trip, and this was the first story I happened to pick up on my return, which was a bit odd, since it was about a would-be suicide and, as it happened, I'd helped to talk a young girl down from a bridge railing while I'd been away.

It was a place I'd visited before, and people had always gone out of their way to be kind to me there. Two or three acquaintances mentioned the new system of walking trails that had been constructed since my last visit. One friend even gave me quite detailed instructions so that I could set out on my own, whenever I had a free moment, without getting lost. One of the longer walks involved crossing what had once been an old railway bridge, though the train no longer used that route. In fact the train now bypassed the town entirely. The bridge had been rebuilt as a wide and sturdy footbridge, though people still referred to it as "the old railway bridge" to distinguish it from other bridges in the area. The town must have suffered somewhat, just as other towns do, at

73

the withdrawal of train services, but the only thing I heard mentioned in this regard was the minor inconvenience of having to pick up visitors by car at the closest functional station in another town an hour and a half away. Most people came by plane anyway, just as I had, though plane services too were in the process of being cut down. So far there were still five flights a day one way or the other, either in or out. It was still a provincial capital after all.

At least two rivers flowed nearby. The big river (the one with the railway bridge) had been named in honour of a favoured saint by the forces that had come to occupy and tame what was once thought of as a wilderness. The smaller river was allowed to keep its native name, as if to commemorate the language once spoken by a now-vanished group. These earlier inhabitants had also once been considered part of the wilderness. In this way the language, and the maps, had become decorated with mutually foreign-sounding words, words that might have seemed antithetical to one another, but together had come to define the linguistic terrain of the region.

I followed the path into the woods, and just as my friend had described, it led across the old railway bridge. The water beneath the bridge was wide and deep and not particularly clear. It seemed to swell as it flowed, as if pushing something unseen downriver. Indeed a large dredging barge was planted in the midst of the river, doing its unseen work. At one point along the right-hand side of the bridge was a bronze plaque, along with three poems and some plastic flowers tacked to the wooden railing. A boy had jumped to his death here some time ago it seemed, and the poems – one by his parents – were there not only to mark the loss, but also as a means of speaking with him directly. The poems, expressed in commonplaces, were not fine art, but they *were* communication. They were the sort of poems that say what they mean. Amazingly, almost superstitiously, people still fall back on writing poetry when they feel they have something truly important to communicate.

I continued across the bridge and entered the woods on the far side and, as promised, it wasn't long til the forest path petered out and a smaller trail began. I decided to turn around. I had just started back across the bridge when I noticed two young girls up ahead. One of them hoisted herself up onto the railing, where she sat facing the river, dangling her legs. They were right at the spot where the poems and flowers had been posted.

During the trip I'd already spoken several times with an old friend whose life had changed. Not so much his external life – it's that something had changed in his heart. Had he been the one to come upon that young girl as she climbed onto the railing, he told me later, he would have done exactly the same as I had, but in his heart he would have been thinking "jump, jump –" because he would have been able to see just by looking that her life would get no better.

Really the problem was simply that the girl had mis-chosen her friends, or so it seemed to me. The one little girl who stood with me as we tried to talk her down was a true friend, but the ones she was thinking of at that moment were those other "friends," who'd said cruel things to taunt her, and driven her out here, onto the top of this railing. Why did she consider them her friends? Why did their friendship take precedence over that of the loyal little girl who stood by her? The two of them looked inconceivably young, but must have been in the sixth or seventh grade.

After some ten or fifteen minutes of talking, the little friend taking part as well, the girl hopped down, slipping into the shoes she'd left neatly beside us. 'Help' is too strong a word for what we did. One never knows what will happen in these cases. All of a sudden a young woman in a sweatshirt appeared beside us as if she'd been waiting in the wings with her breath held all this time, and thanked me, and led the girls away.

But those poems, as far as I know, are still on the bridge: a symbol, and a magnet for kids who can see no way out of their difficulties. In making offerings to the past there can be nothing to gain. The past is the past. Yet it is also the present and the future: it is that aspect of the present and future that cannot be affected by anything we do. My friend was right. When I shook the young girl's hand after she'd come down off the railing she looked right into my eyes, and then looked down again as the woman in the sweatshirt swept her away with the other little girl. It was as if the river had taken her. I don't even remember her name.

As for the boy who died, my friend told me it was actually an accident. It seems he'd been drunk, and trying to walk the bridge railing as a stunt for an admiring group of friends. Maybe the family of the dead boy should take the poems and flowers down. Maybe they should try speaking to him in their hearts instead of in poems meant to be seen in public places. Maybe in that way they might honour the living, and save death for the dead, and say whatever it is they have to say in a way that will do no harm and where no one will overhear. As for the words I said to the little girl, I know she won't think of them, but I still hope they'll surface when they're most needed. Even if they're not true, even if they, like all words, were just a manipulation of the truth. The truth is, I wanted her to come down off that bridge. I wanted to think that I could come from the big city where she'd never been, and look into her eyes, and tell her that the world was wider than she imagined, and that it was possible to make better friends. I wanted our eyes to make the pact that friends make, and for which we would be willing to live.

I understand the parents' wish, despite everything, to speak to their son, though if it were up to me I'd take the poems and flowers down. Yet I too would like to place a poem on the bridge for those who've gone under, as well as those of us who've stayed above.

On the last night of the year
the swans set sail at evening.
Then among the boats and fireworks
we can see the black water,
the city in the river.
That's where all our life is,
beyond the grief and failure,
the wake among the reeds.

Down there
down there
what is that place now
but a hill studded with lights
and a pine tree that doesn't move with the wind?
Wherever there is summer,
wherever the crickets sing to it,
that place is.
But longing is a wind that blows through you,
and like the pine that is nowhere
you do not move.

UPRIVER TOWARD ŌISHIDA

A friend's poem reads: "We left the city, moving to this coast and its cooler climate when I turned fifty and wanted to change my life." Nearing the age of 50, and feeling similar urges, I too imagine places it might be pleasant to move to, and tiring of the small world that is poetry, perhaps in this too wishing to "change my life," find myself drifting back to reading works of literature I first read years or decades earlier, seeing that former self as if it were a figure set before me in some record from another time.

Bashō was born in 1644, near Ueno in Iga Province, and at the age of 28 set out for Edo, apparently aiming to make a name for himself in poetry. The move, presumably, did not go well at first, for little is known of his first eight years in Edo. Arriving there, it seems he worked for a time in the local waterworks, his mood swinging back and forth between periods of despair, in which he resolved to give up poetry, and others in which he determined to go on writing, certain he would one day become famous above all others. "These two possibilities," he wrote, "battled in my mind, and made my life restless."

Reading these lines, I feel unexpectedly sunny. It occurs to me that I too, feeling sorry for myself, have already "given up" poetry twice – to which poetry replied by supplying a silly riddle:

> Throw it away,
> it comes back.

> Throw it away harder,
> it still comes back.

Knowing no Japanese, I've read Bashō only in translation. I'm as ignorant as the crows and carp, who neither read nor write, and so know nothing of the medieval poetry of which their ancestors were so often the subjects. You can't know poetry without knowing the language. Still,

81

now and then, scanning the original text, I come across familiar Chinese characters. They seem stranded there, as if deposited by some long-since-departed glacier. But isn't this feeling, which arises from poetry, the ongoing feeling of life itself? Don't the crows and the carp also have this feeling? For me, it's possible to recognize those characters, even to be able to read them aloud (albeit in Chinese, not in Japanese), without being able to reproduce them for myself. To learn to write, one must practise endlessly, tracing *shuǐ*, the character for water, for example, at every opportunity – in tea spilled on a restaurant table, the condensation on a glass of ice-cold water brought out in the middle of a summer afternoon, the steam on the inside of a shower door. Only in this way will the arm come to learn the necessary movements on its own.

Writing, as Jane Austen knew, is easily hidden under a scrap of embroidery, but requires that kind of stubborn practice. I lean over my desk and daydream, settling into a posture my long-ago physiotherapist would never have approved of. Cupping my shoulders in her hands she'd try to coax them into new positions, both of us knowing I wouldn't be able to maintain these on my own. In the same way Bashō corrected the poems brought to him by others. He acted, rather than trying to explain or uselessly elaborate.

A hundred years ago in China, those who were meant to read and write had to learn by sheer memorization. A pupil would be given a certain portion of the classics, his teacher pronouncing aloud any unfamiliar characters. The next day the pupil would be expected to recite the passage by heart as well as to be able to write it out without error. No further clarification would be given. It was only through ceaseless practice and repetition that the student might gradually come to understand the meaning of the individual words as well as of the passage as a whole. Read and write, the method seemed to say, and ultimately you will understand.

Sora and his friend Bashō travelled together through Ōishida, which lies on the Mogami River. According to the map, the Mogami River begins in Michinoku Province and flows first north toward Obanazawa, then west toward Sakata and the sea. Ōishida lies halfway along the northward section, on the northernmost stretch of the journey described in Bashō's *Narrow Road to the Deep North*. According to Bashō, the party, having decided to take a boat downriver, stopped for a few days at Ōishida, awaiting fair weather. There, pressed by the villagers, who did not wish to let pass the opportunity afforded by the visit of so famous a poet, he recorded: "We joined them in composing several poems – enough for a small volume – which we left behind. It is in this way that my journey has brought the style I practise to even so remote an area as this." Later he added:

> Gathering the fifth-month's rains,
> how swiftly flows
> the Mogami River.

Sora too left a diary of the trip, though as is well known, the entries don't agree in every respect with those of the *Narrow Road*. Sora abandoned the journey at one point, or rather went off in his own direction (Bashō records that he fell ill with abdominal trouble, and had to go on ahead to relatives at Nagashima). Later in the journey Bashō stops at places where Sora has preceded him and left poems – but at Ōishida, in the rainy season, they were together. It's not necessary to account for any discrepancies. Even a master such as Bashō could do no better than to write down the words that came to him, and later rearrange them.

Shortly after rereading *Narrow Road to the Deep North*, I had one of those strange half-conscious dreams that occur just before waking. One moment a friend was showing slides of his latest trip, providing the usual type of casual commentary, and the next, the friend had become Bashō, and the trip his journey to the far north. One after another, on the wall of our living room, scenes of "Japan" appeared, a Japan I've never been to ... *My old grass hut/abandoned but for dolls/ is lived in by another generation ... not even five feet in dimension – / I might have knocked it down for kindling/had it not kept me from the rain ... the little boats of the fishermen/row in at dusk ... the babble of voices as they divide their catch ... and the sky, from which summer rain has been falling,/clears, and near at hand/the darkened forms of islands loom up ... After much looking we found an old shed/and having spent the night there cold and miserable/set out again the next morning, travelling at random over unknown roads ... fleas and lice/and the sound of pissing horses/much disturbed our sleep ... Today I sat for a while/and was comforted by idleness ... then we passed the most dangerous part of our journey/places with names like Deserting-Parents-Abandoned-Children,/Excluded-Dog and Rejected-Horse./Tired from our exertions,/we took a bed in the first inn we came to for the night/and lay down to rest,/but two young women were/ laughing quietly together in a room nearby,/the sound of their voices mingling now and then with that of an old man ... It is written that Kurobe has 48 rapids – /I do not know how many we crossed,/but we came at last to the ocean/and a place called Nago Bay ... The next day was the 16th, and the sky had cleared at last./Thinking I would like to go hunting for the famous little coloured clams,/I hired a boat to take me to the beach at Iro ... that night I had a dream in which a willow tree that had once been the priest Saigyō appeared,/and it occurred to me that I would wake in the morning without bitterness ...* But if you can trust what you see in dreams, it is no longer there.

> The willow is gone,
> and a small pool, instead,
> gathers the rain.

When I awoke, it was April. I had just turned 49 and, feeling suddenly old, I realized that at this age Bashō would have already set out on his last journey, the one from which he would not return. The night rain had torn the blossoms from the trees. But which April was it, the southern or the northern? Autumn or spring? I was reminded of something that happened long ago, to the person I used to be. Still a student, one day I walked into my dormitory room to find the narrow bed covered in petals. A young man had sneaked in, and then out again, leaving this old idea as a surprise. There was no note. I knew who had left them, but I was not in love with him. I sat down, clearing a small space for myself, and opening the book I'd been carrying, began to read. It was an old poem by Meng Haoran, which begins:

> Springtime: I sleep late, and so no longer feel the dawn.
> Everywhere the chattering of birds –

and ends:

> at night the sounds of wind and rain.
> Flowers fall. Who knows how many.

Maybe this is what Bashō, who knew the work of the old Tang poets well, was echoing when he wrote:

> When I woke, after much late-night drinking and a long sleep, the
> first day of the new year was already half-gone.
>
> > Tomorrow, if it is not already too late,
> > I will get up early
> > and welcome in the new spring blossoms.

Bashō was 45 – "still young," that is – when he set out on the journey described in the *Narrow Road to the Deep North*. Later he wrote: "Whenever people come, there is more pointless talk; whenever I go to visit, the unhealthy feeling of interfering in the business of other men."

As he lay on his deathbed in Ōsaka, disciples from around the country hurried to his side. To his older brother he wrote: "It is sad to leave you now. I hope you live a happy life and reach a ripe old age." Through all of this, he continued to write. Asked by his friend Kyorai if the poem

> Sick on my journey
> my thoughts wander aimlessly
> over the blighted moor

should be considered his *jisei*, or death poem, Bashō insisted it should not. "If anyone asks," he told Kyorai, "tell them that *all* my everyday poems should be considered my *jisei*." As always, the records disagree. In one it is said that his obsessive writing left no time for final prayers, in another that, just before death, he clasped his hands together and recited what sounded like a passage from the sutras. Yet another, which I prefer, reports that his last words were: "Those flies certainly *enjoy* having a dying man around."

If once I would have wanted a master such as Bashō, now I'm no longer so sure. It's said he was ruthless when it came to poetry, whether his own or others'. Thus when he instructed his disciples to compose a final poem in his honour – with the warning that he did not want to have to revise so much as a single syllable of it – those who stood nearest, I imagine, wouldn't have known whether to be moved by this last request or terrified.

Ōishida still exists on the map. I would someday like to go there. Whether it would be the same Ōishida Bashō knew is another question. Nonetheless I would like to walk the streets and see for myself. There are places one cannot go except in literature, but then again there is a version of time which literature, and all ordinary human commerce, keeps us from. In that version, Bashō's Ōishida no longer exists – but fortunately, poetry keeps intervening, poetry and its obsession with the "qualities" of things, the huts of the fishermen on the beach, the little coloured clams, and so on.

But these, as always, are technical matters, and best not dwelt on. It is as though, all those long years ago, you rose at last from the cool night grass and set out, just as you remember,

> Early in the morning or else past sundown,
> at evening, dusk,
> the wind through the open window,
> the radio on and the unopened map beside you –

NOTES AND ACKNOWLEDGEMENTS

The Torrens, Patawalonga, Onkaparinga, and Little Para are the "four celebrated rivers" of the Adelaide Hills and Plains in South Australia. Mt. Lofty, in the Mount Lofty Ranges, rises to the southeast of the city of Adelaide.

The Earl Miner quote near the end of "Autumn Record" is from his *Japanese Poetic Diaries* (University of California Press, 1969).

The epigraph leading into the five pieces of the section "Water Colour" is by Andy Patton, from an unpublished letter.

"Upriver Toward Ōishida": The quote from "a friend's poem" is borrowed from the title poem of Jane Munro's *Point No Point*. A number of sources were consulted regarding Bashō's life and work; chief among these are *Matsuo Bashō* by Makoto Ueda (Twayne, 1970) and *The Narrow Road to the Deep North and Other Travel Sketches* by Nobuyuki Yuasa (Penguin Books, 1966), as well as the aforementioned work by Earl Miner. Much of the 'slide show commentary' is composed of variations on fragments of existing (and wildly varying) translations; however, the felicitous names of the three dangerous places remain in Earl Miner's English. The translation of Meng Haoran's "Spring Dawn" is by Kim Maltman.

"Persimmons" and "Upriver Toward Ōishida" were first published in *Brick*, "Autumn Record," "Spring Cherries," and "Seven Variations on the Word Silk" in *The Capilano Review*, "Summer River" in *Malahat Review*, "Garden" in *Conversations* (Green College), and a portion of "Summer Grass" in *Books in Canada*.

The generous support of a number of organizations has made this work possible: the Canada Council for the Arts, the Ontario Arts Council, Massey College and the Department of English at the University of Toronto, and Green College at the University of British Columbia.

Thanks to my long-time collaborator, Kim Maltman, for extensive editing and rethinking at numerous stages in the composition of this book. Also to Don McKay, for his careful reading and numerous useful suggestions, and to André Alexis, Robert Bringhurst, Dale Estey, Leah Goldman, Janice Gurney, Dennis Lee, Jane Munro, Andy Patton, and Jan Zwicky.

A special debt is owed to the writers mentioned in these pages, and to the translators who have brought their work into English. Such debts can never be repaid – only passed on.